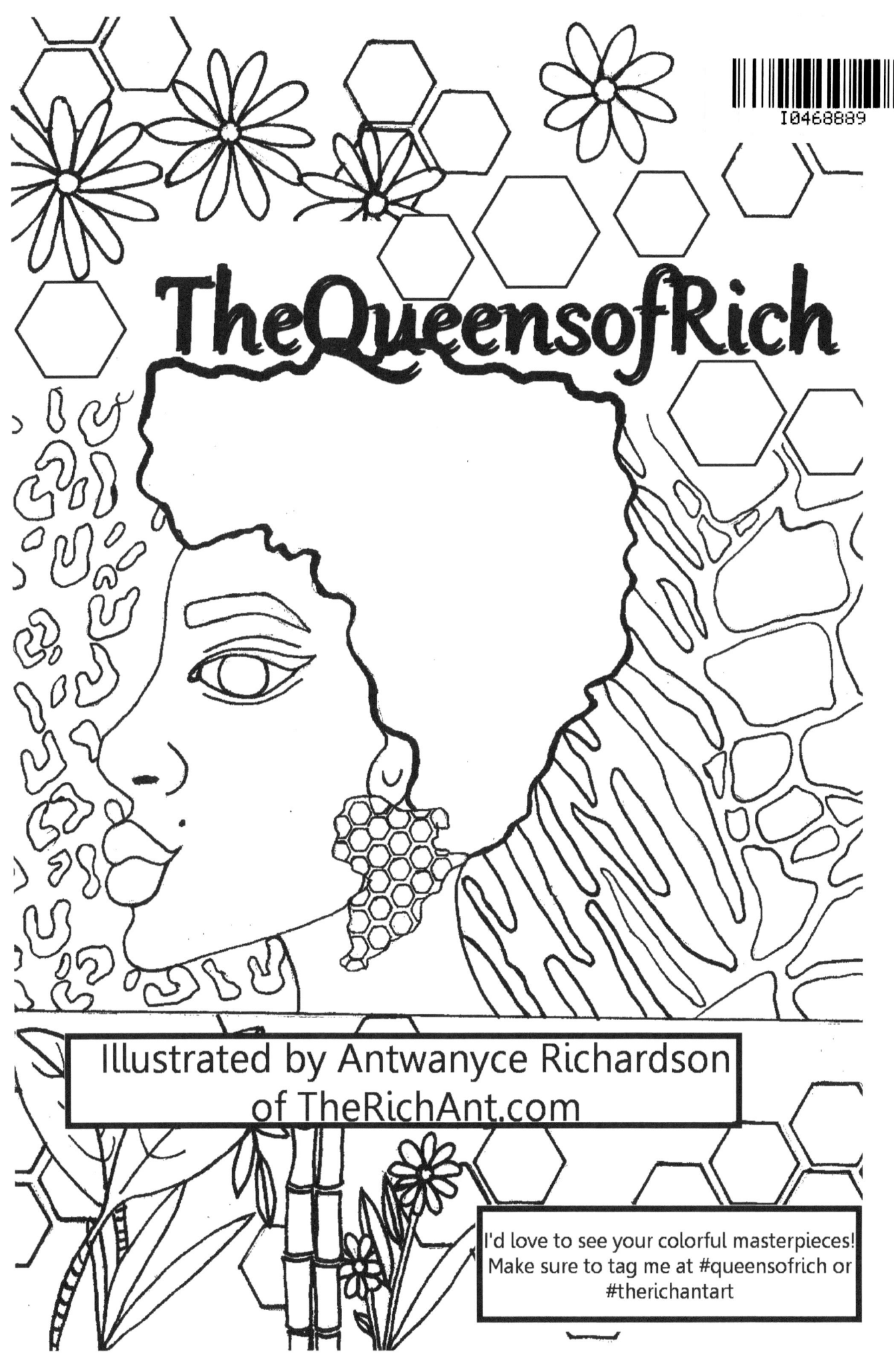

TheQueensofRich

Illustrated by Antwanyce Richardson
of TheRichAnt.com

I'd love to see your colorful masterpieces!
Make sure to tag me at #queensofrich or
#therichantart

I0468889

Antwanyce Richardson is a mixed media visual artist and illustrator who creates paintings and drawings inspired by surrealism, hair, beauty and fashion. With her background in cosmetology and a growing up with a fashion designer mother she creates rich beautiful artworks showcasing women of color.

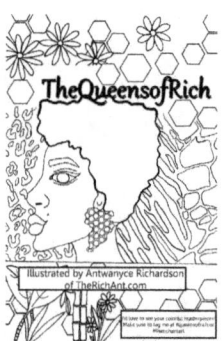

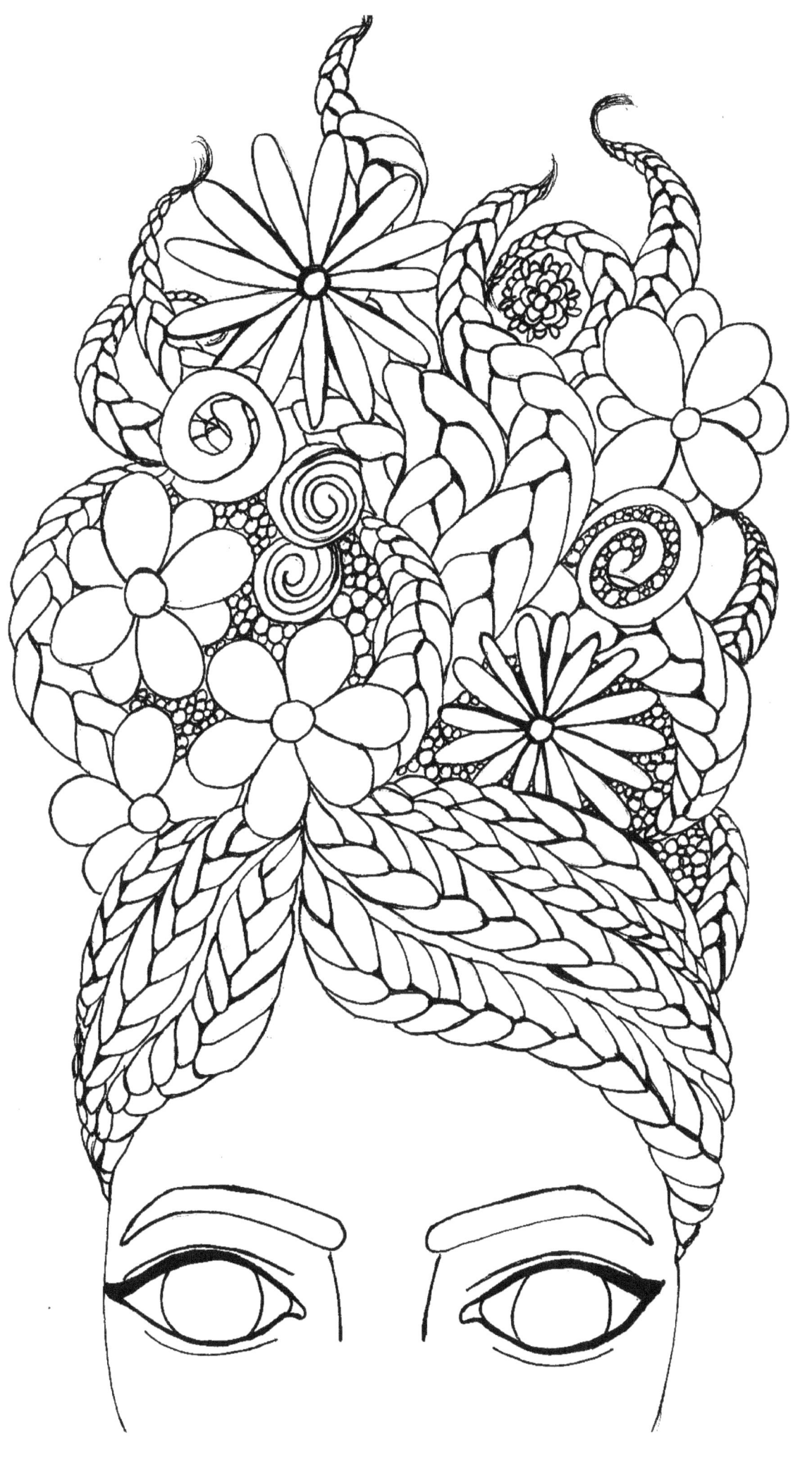

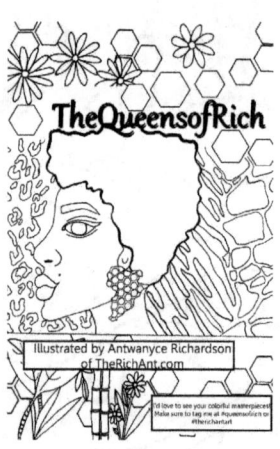

TheQueensofRich

Illustrated by Antwanyce Richardson
of TheRichAnt.com

I'd love to see your colorful masterpiece!
Make sure to tag me at #queensofrich or
#therichertart

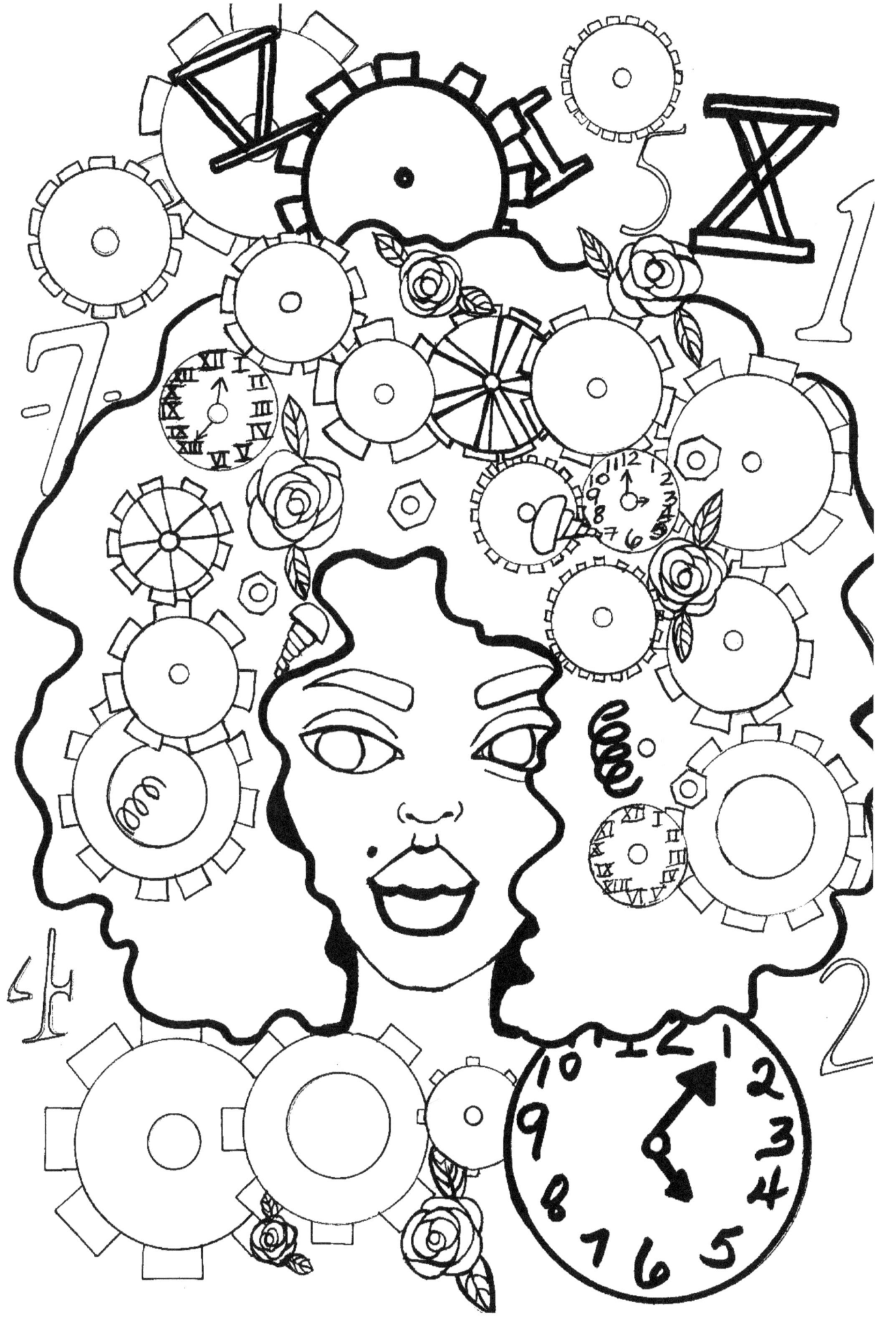

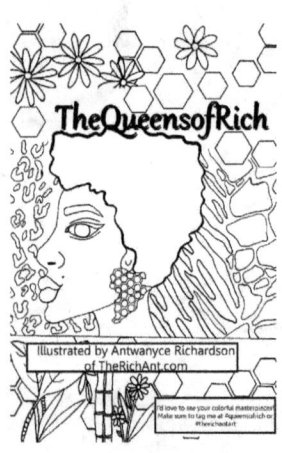

TheQueensofRich

Illustrated by Antwanyce Richardson
of TheRichAnt.com

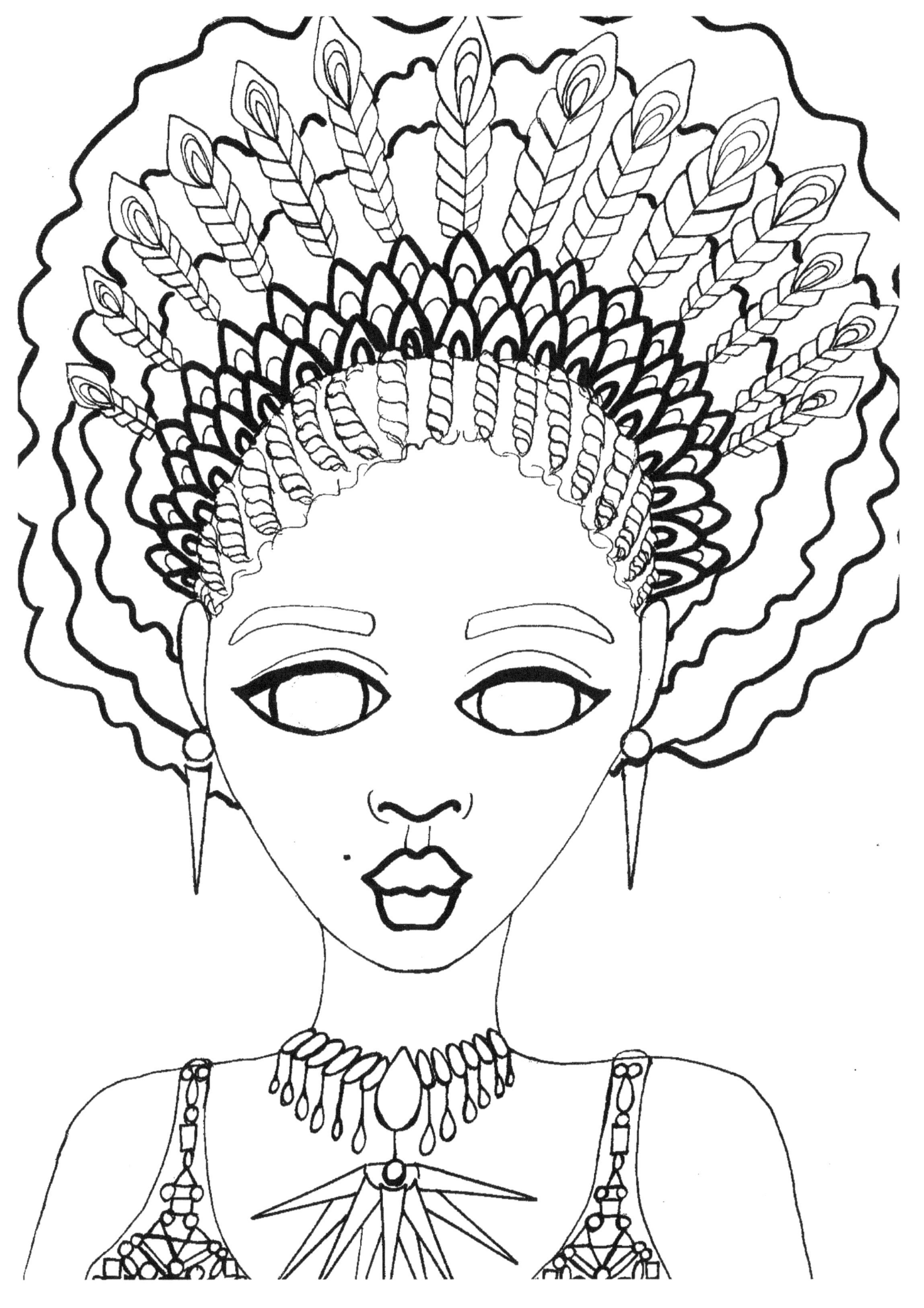

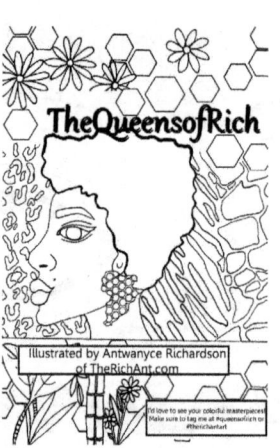

TheQueensofRich

Illustrated by Antwanyce Richardson
of TheRichAnt.com

I'd love to see your colorful masterpieces!
Make sure to tag me at thequeensofrich or
#therichantart

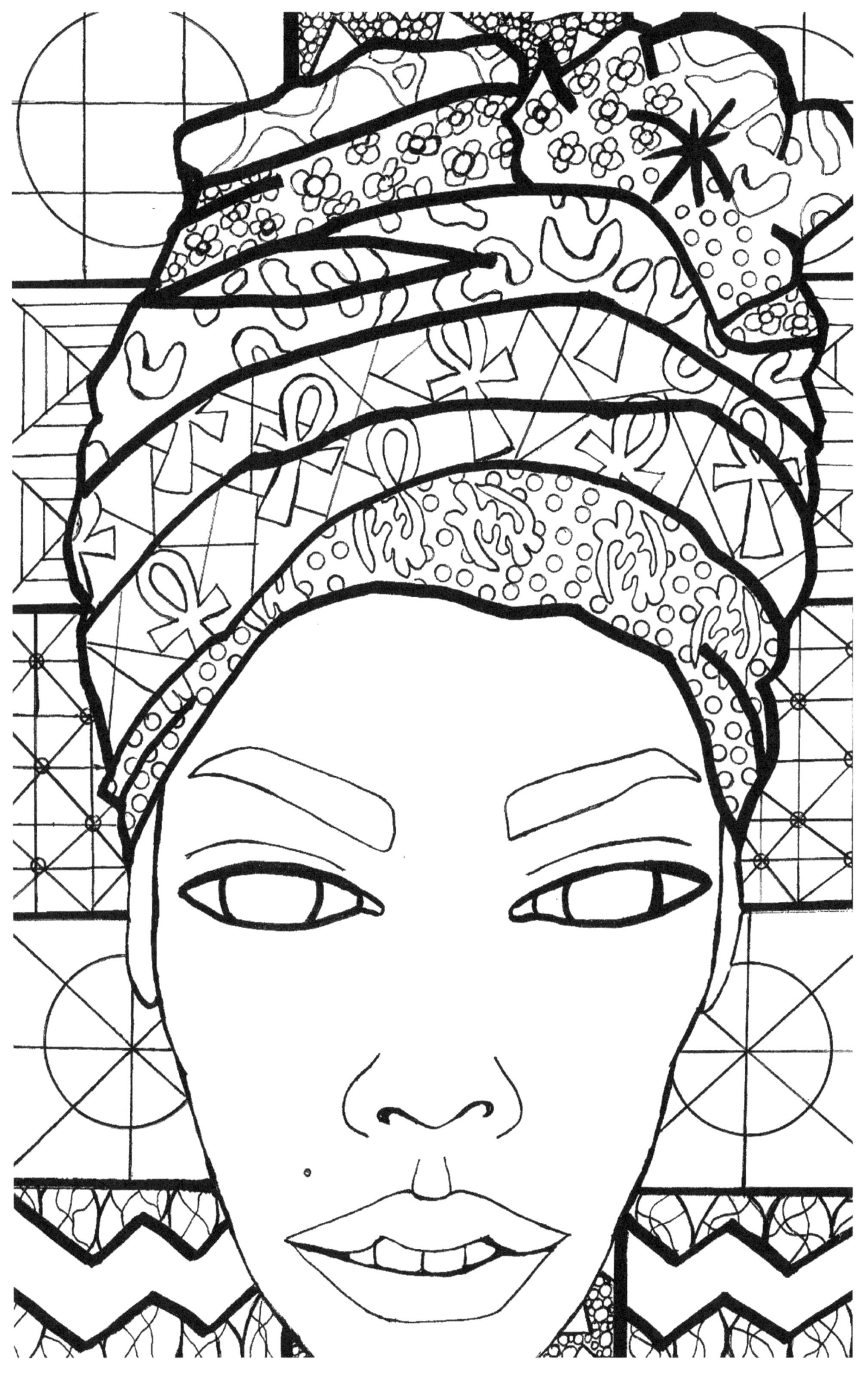

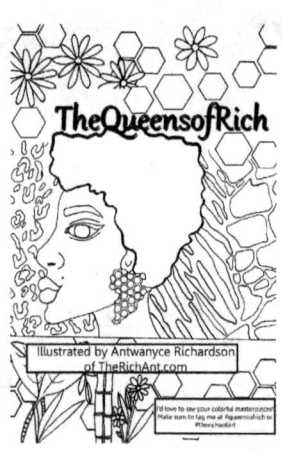

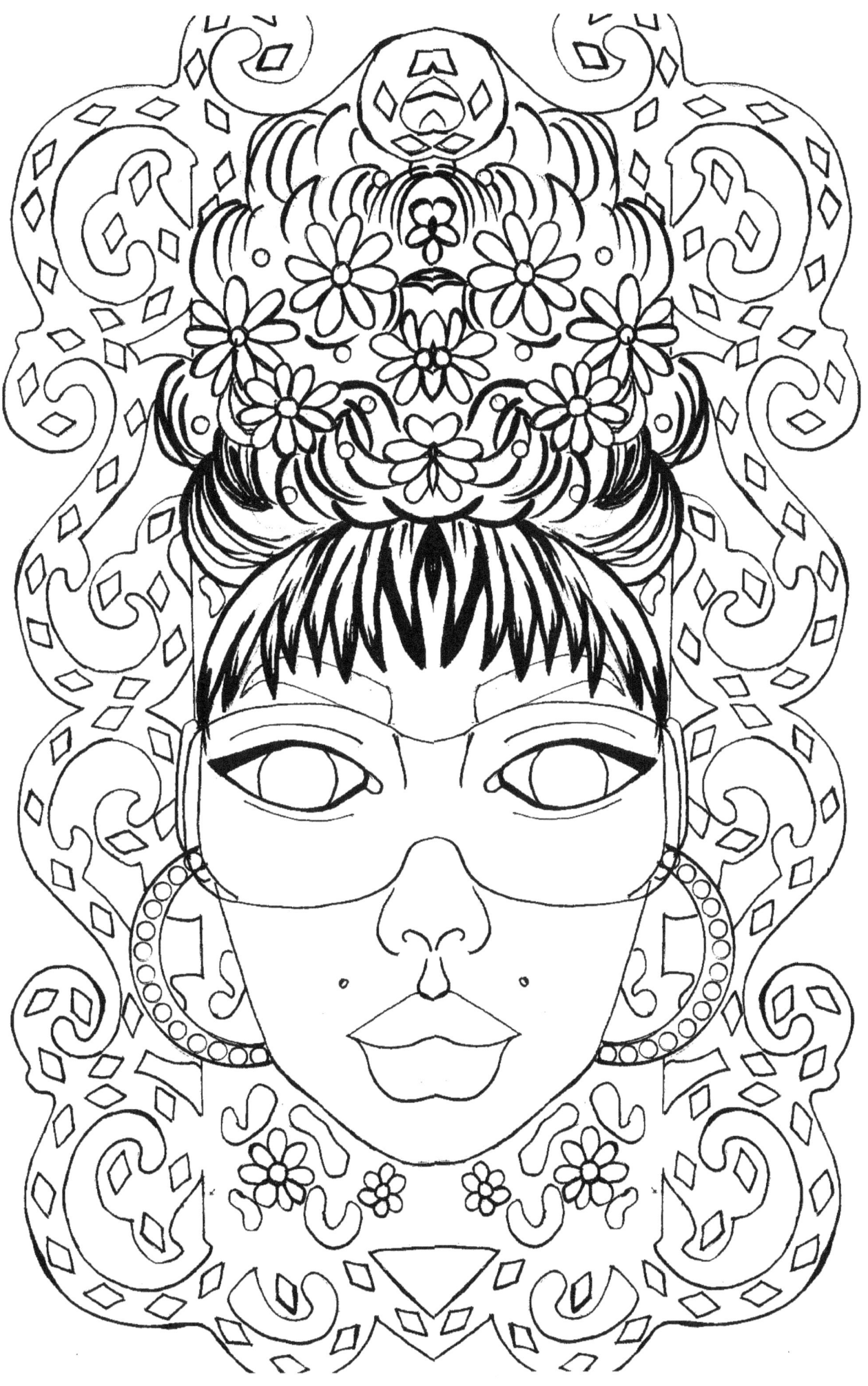

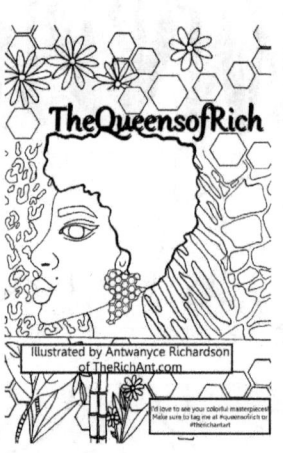

TheQueensofRich

Illustrated by Antwanyce Richardson
of TheRichAnt.com

I'd love to see your colorful masterpieces!
Make sure to tag me at #queensofrich or
#therichantart!

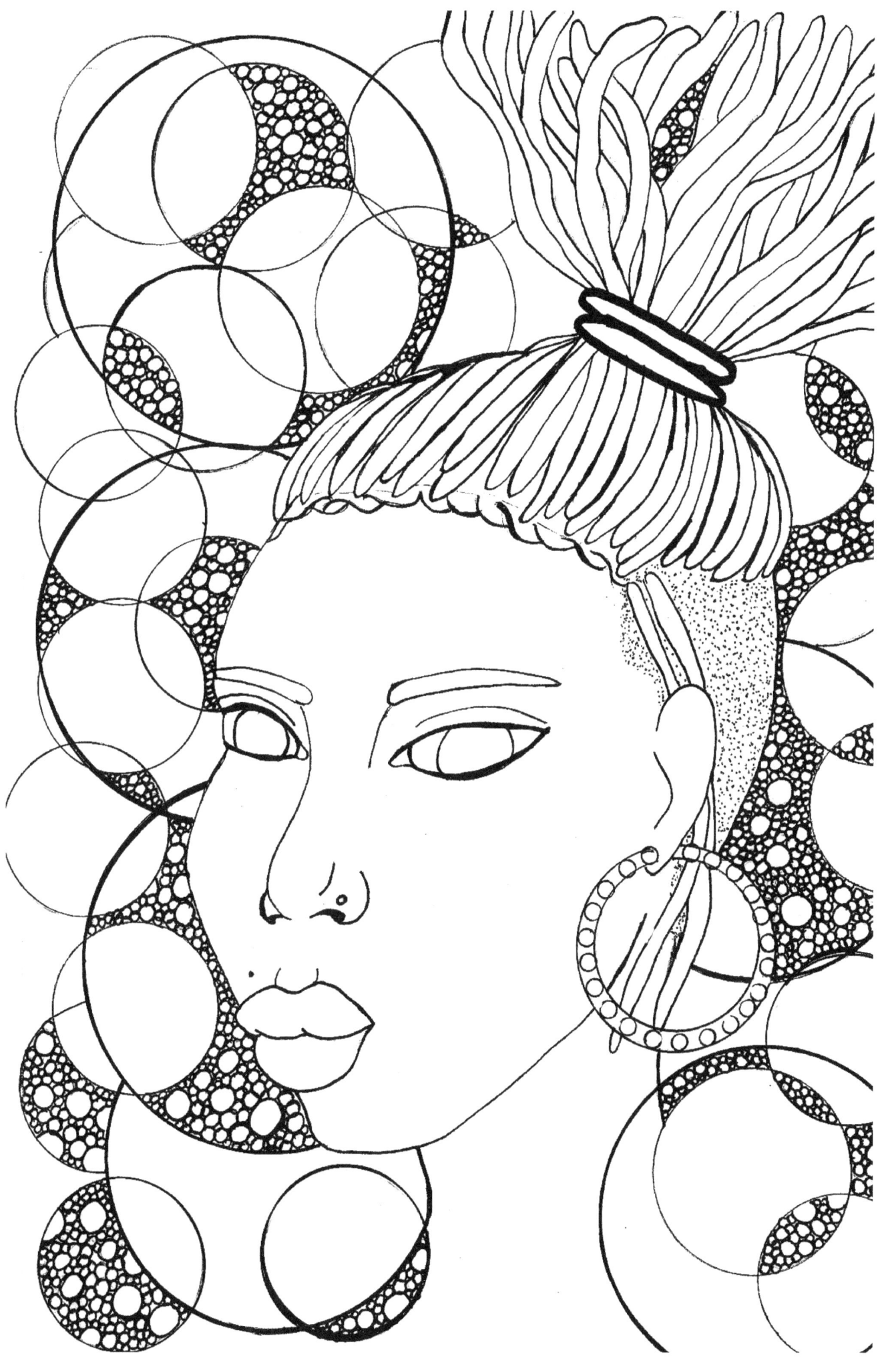

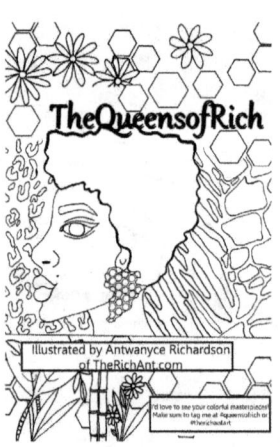

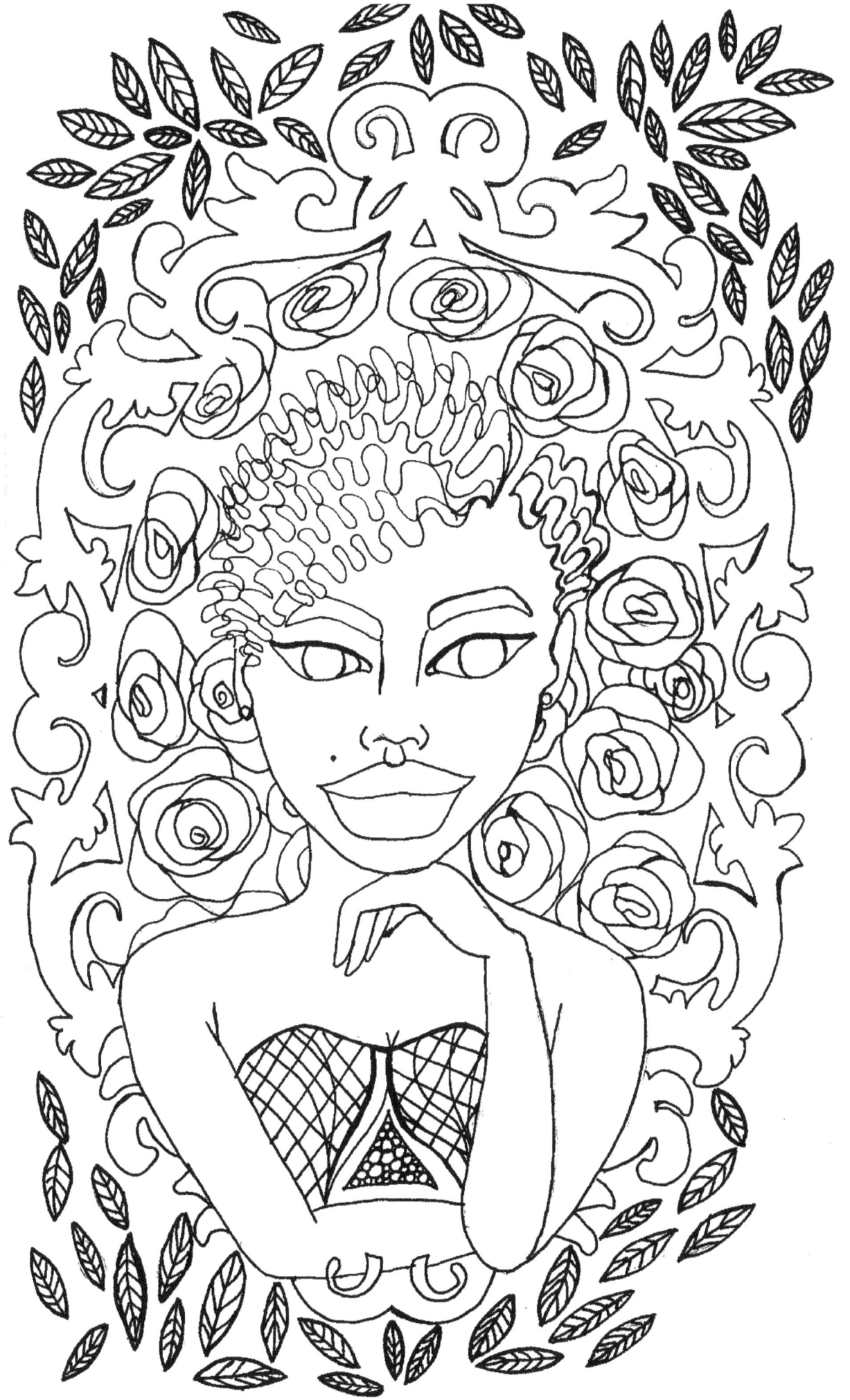

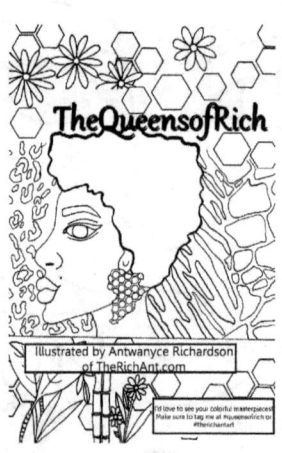

The Queens of Rich

Illustrated by Antwanyce Richardson
of TheRichAnt.com

I'd love to see your colorful masterpieces!
Make sure to tag me at #queensofrich or
#therichantart!

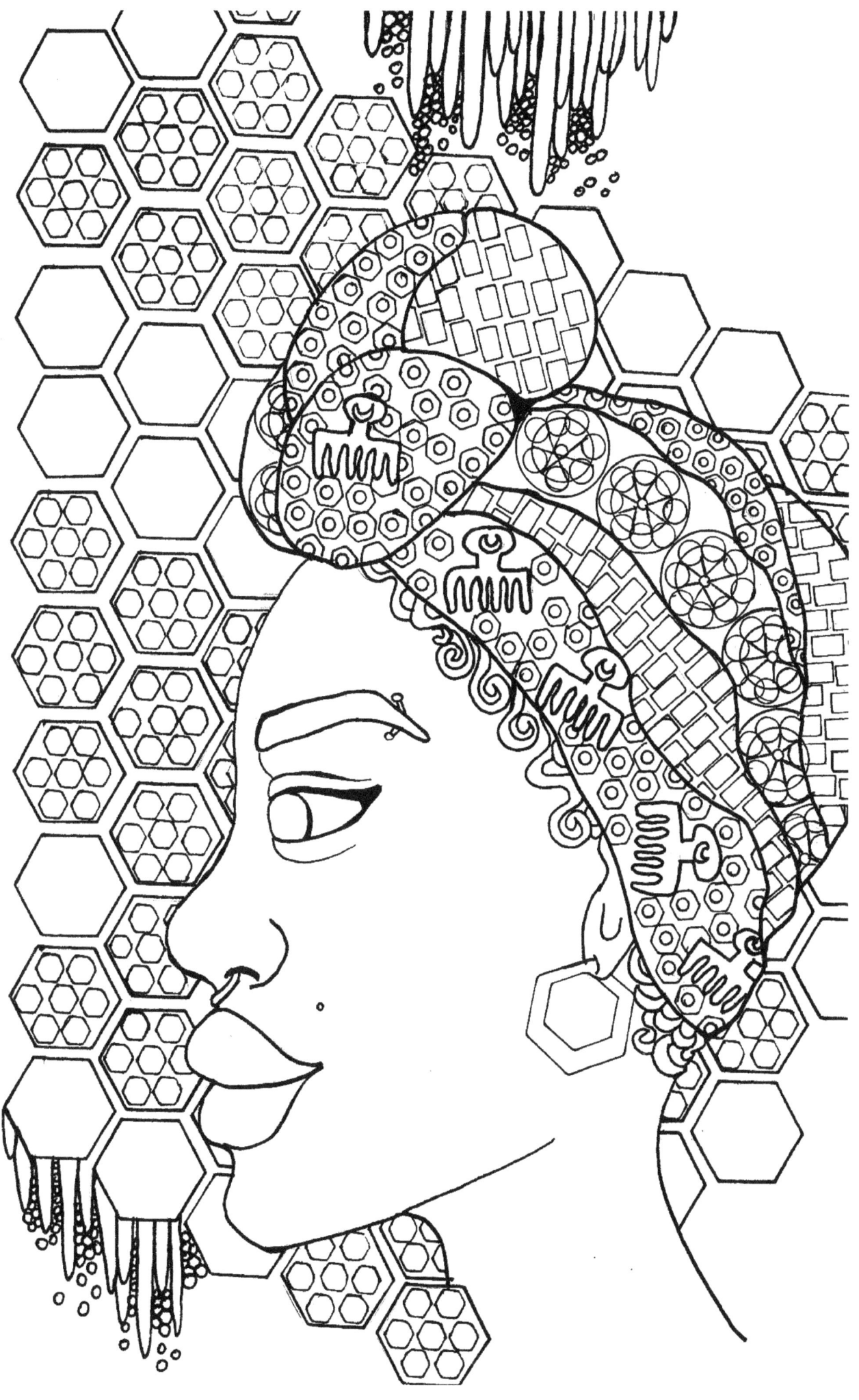

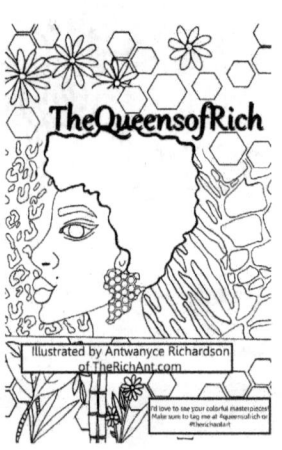

TheQueensofRich

Illustrated by Antwanyce Richardson
of TheRichAnt.com

I'd love to see your colorful masterpiece!
Make sure to tag me at @queensofrich or
#therichantart

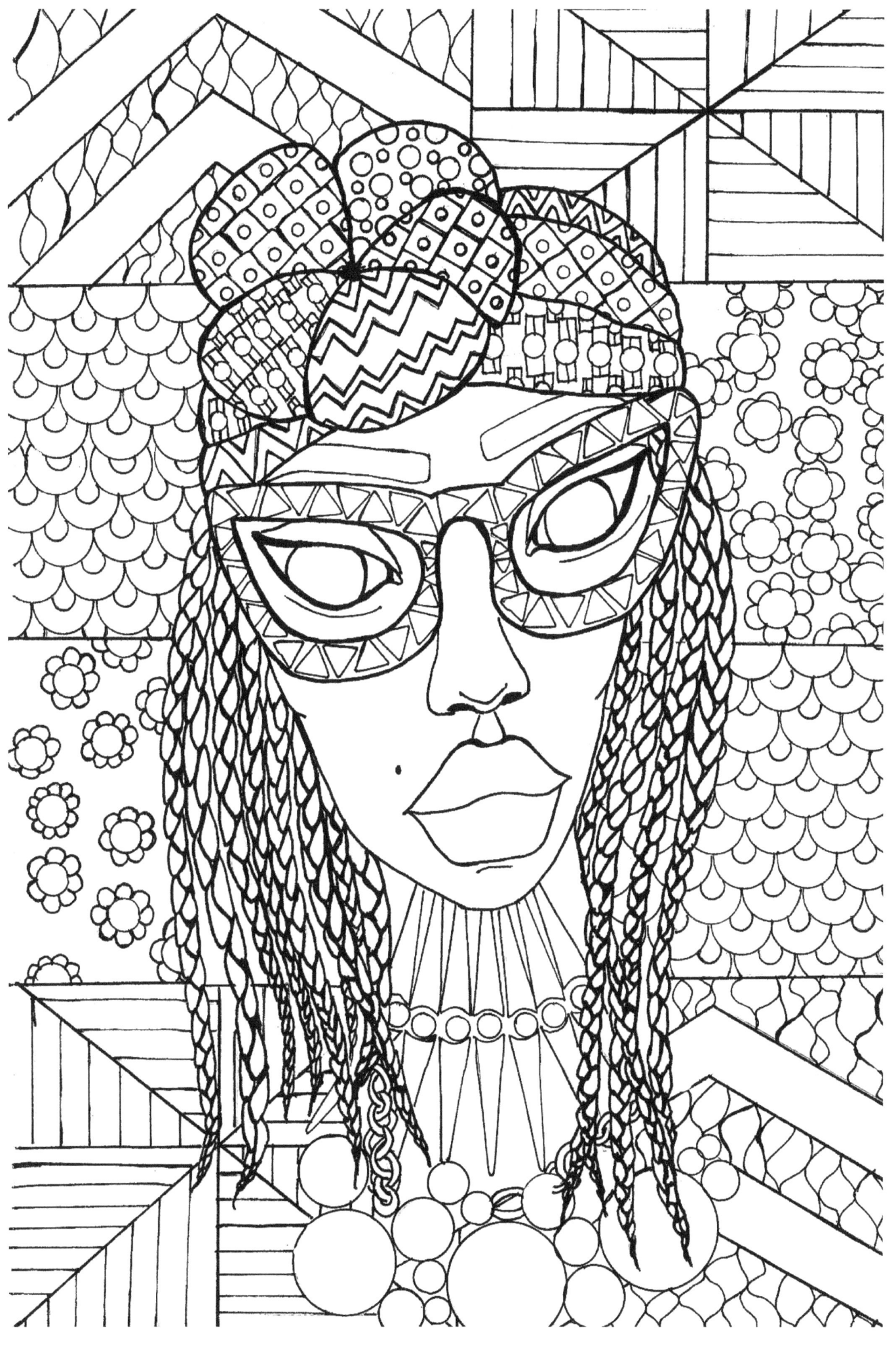

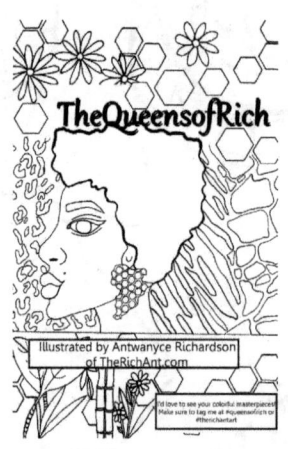

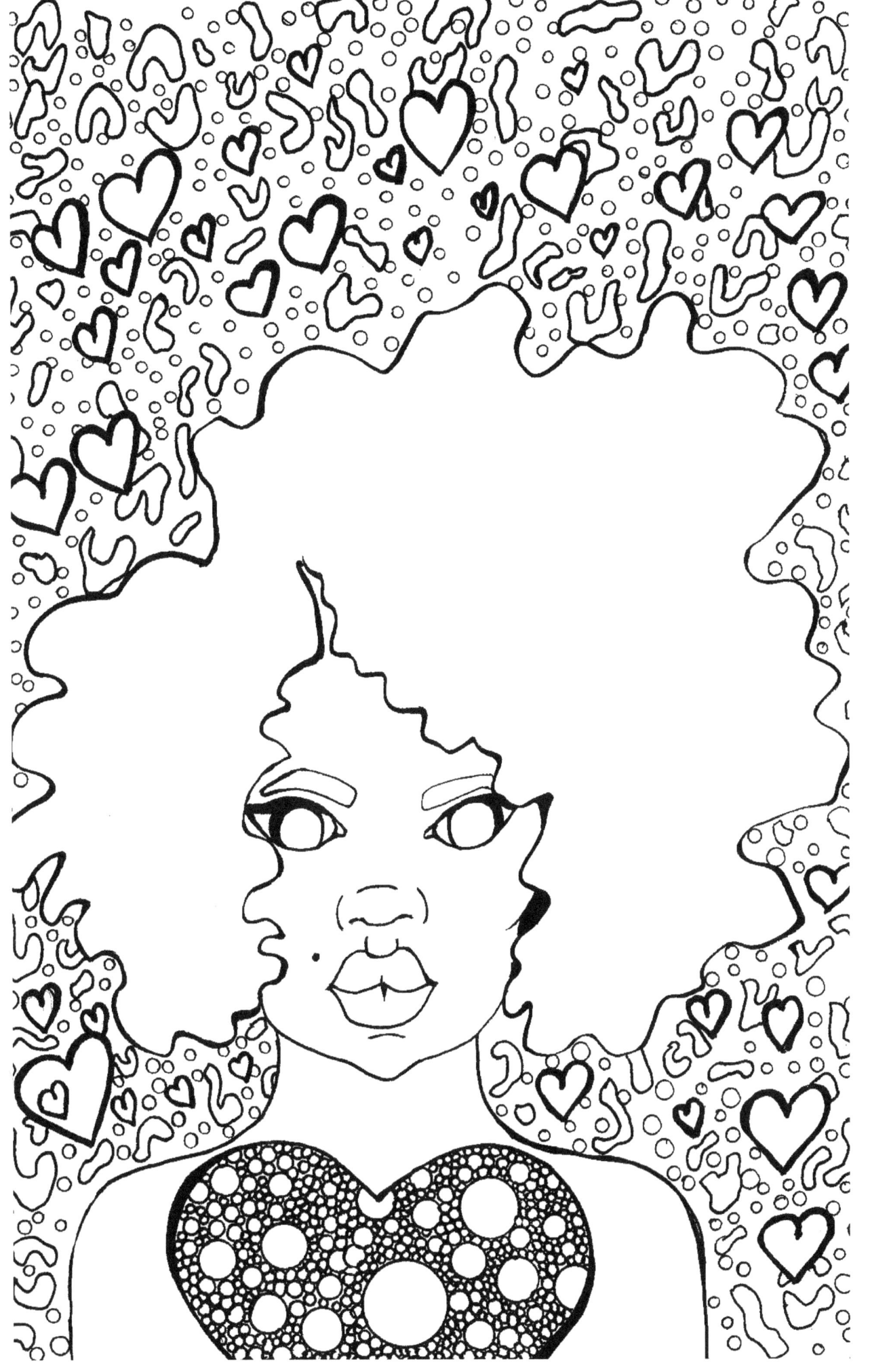

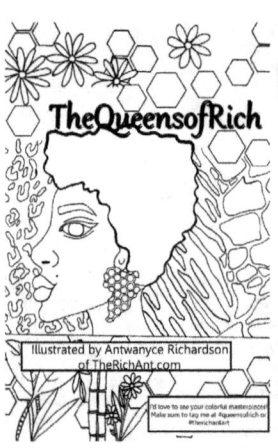

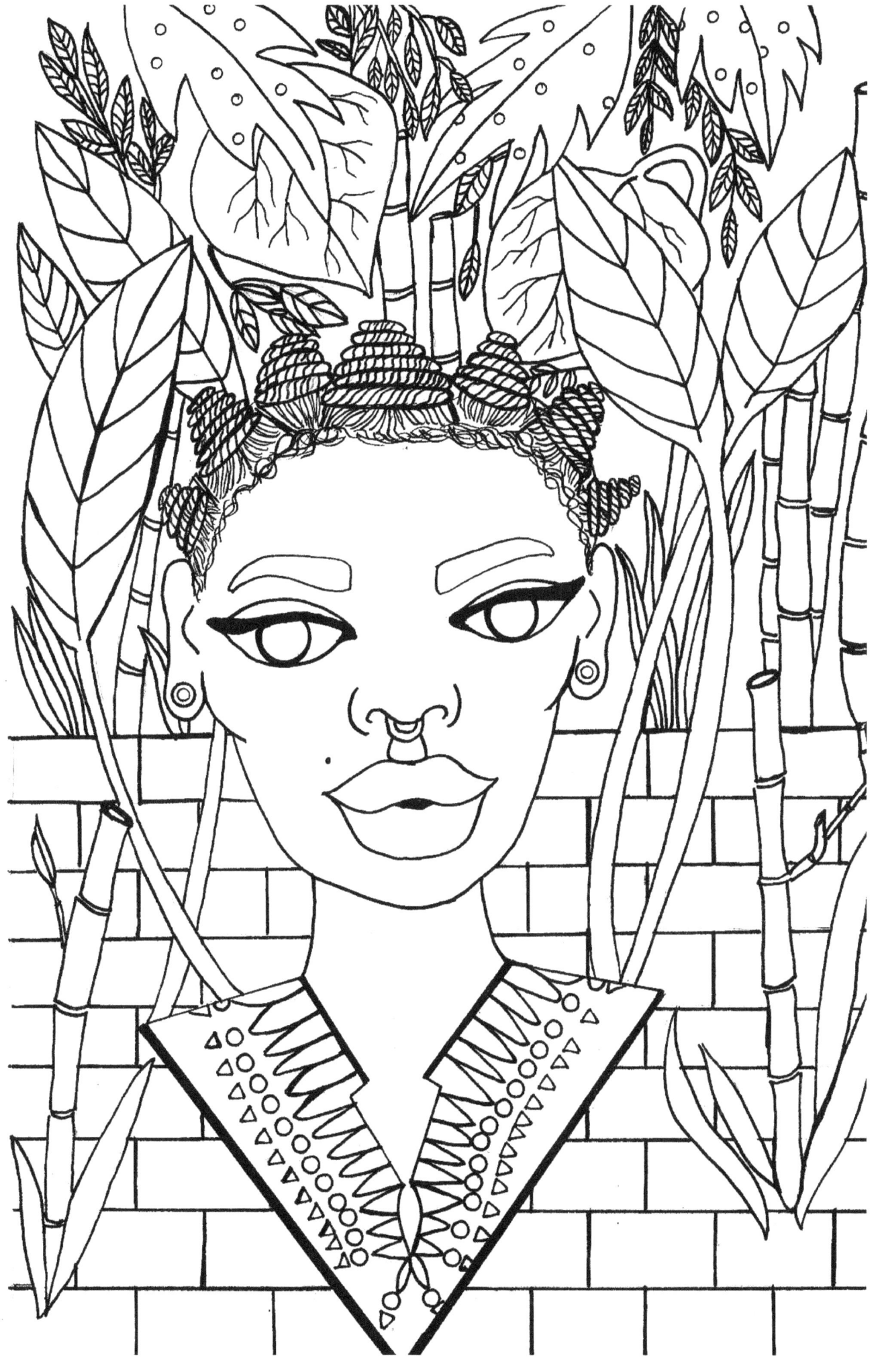

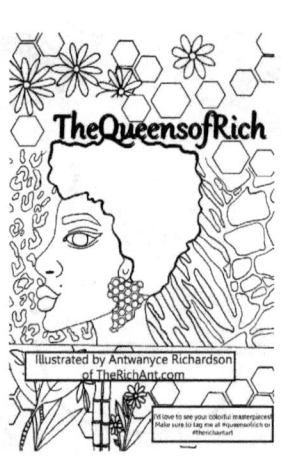

The Queens of Rich

Illustrated by Antwanyce Richardson
of TheRichAnt.com

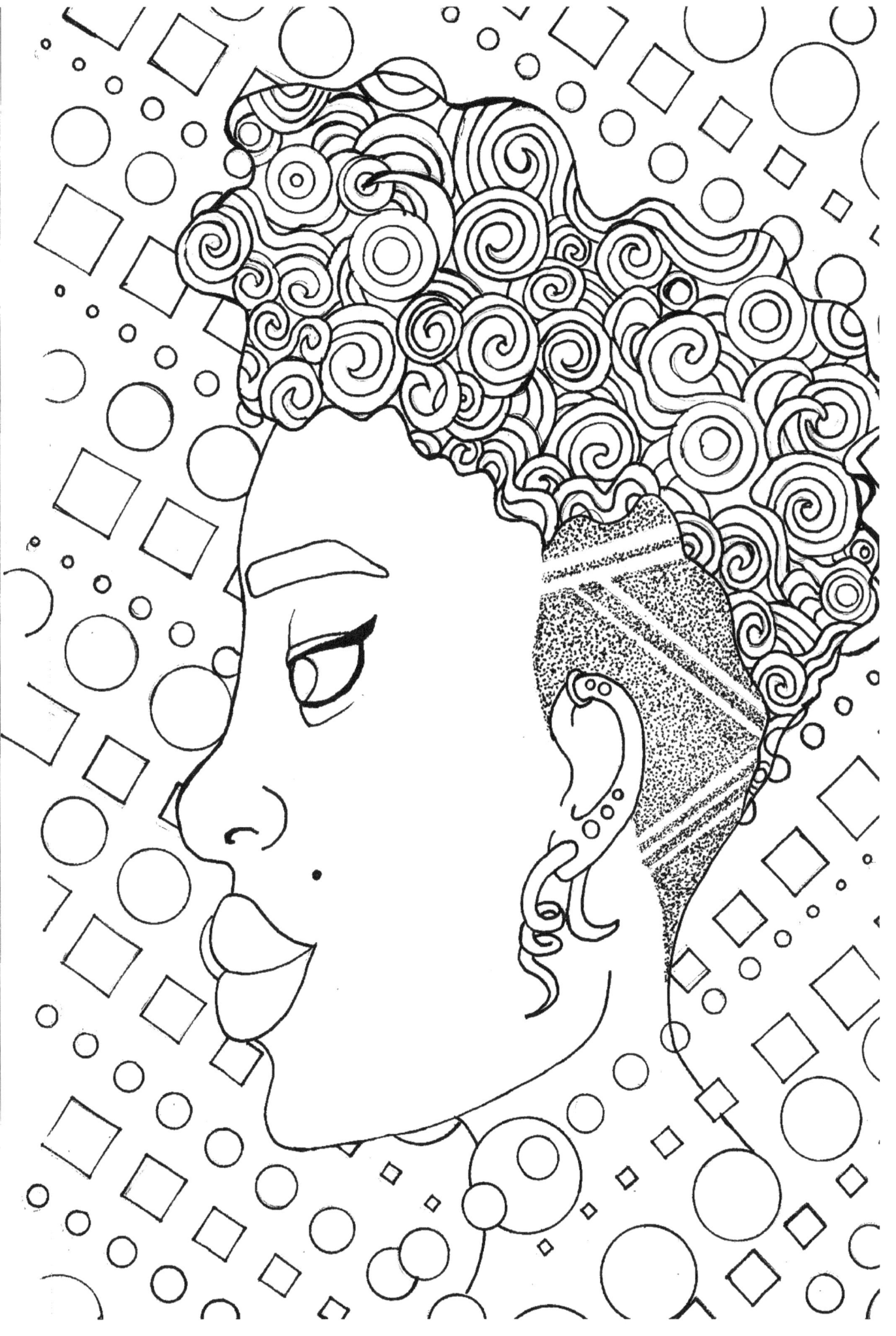

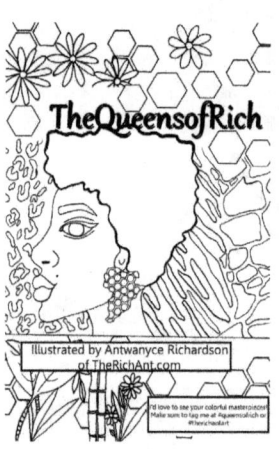

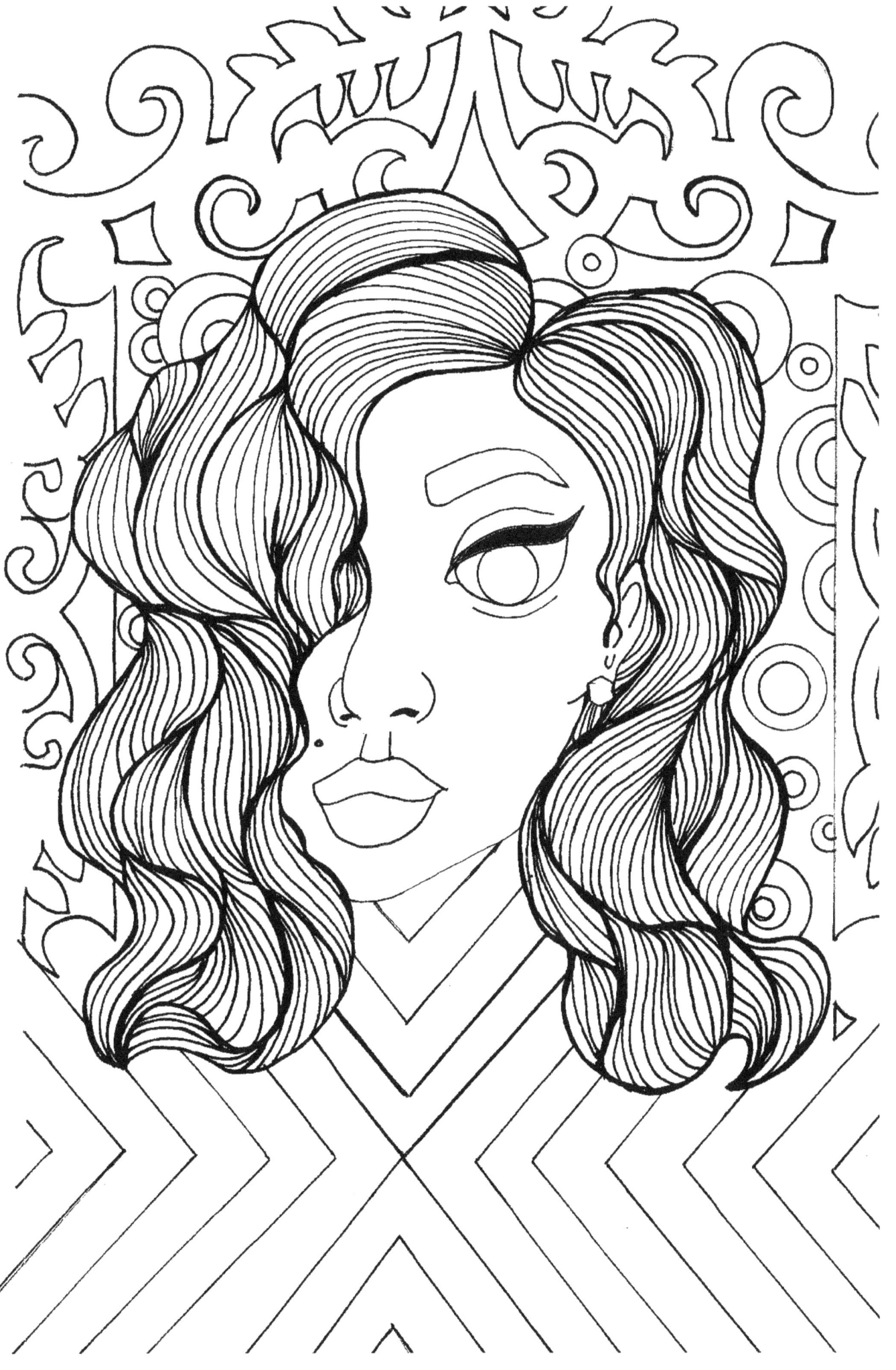

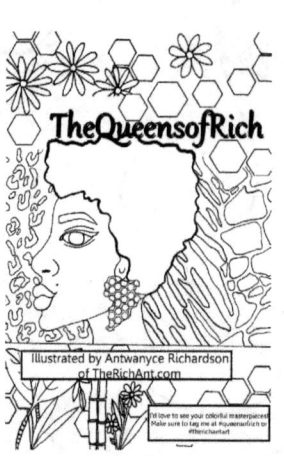

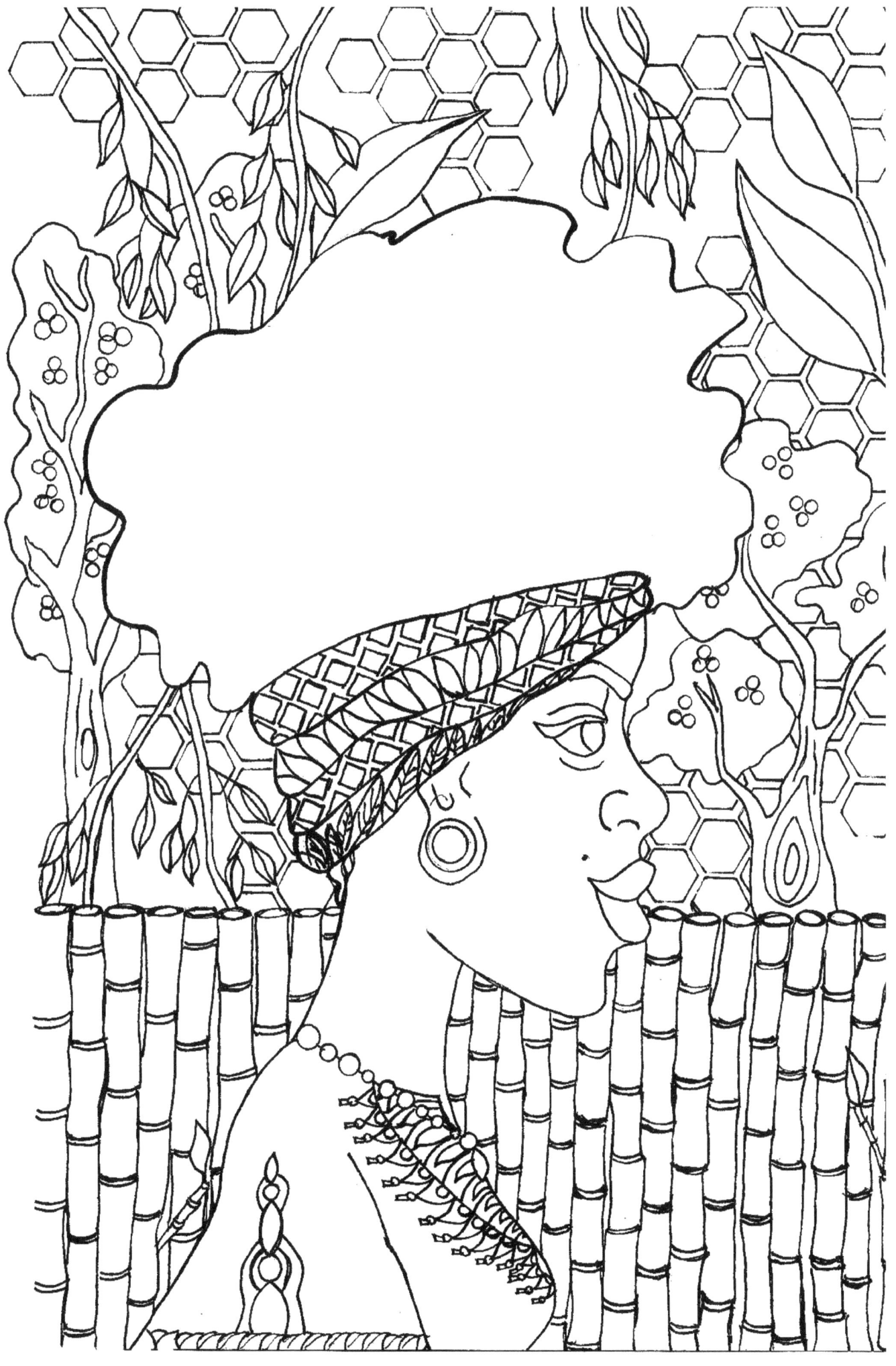

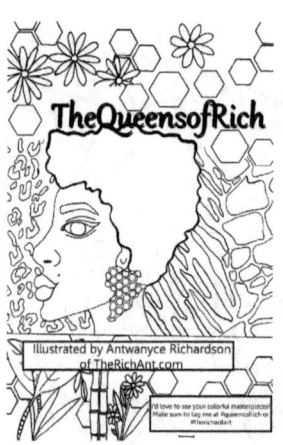

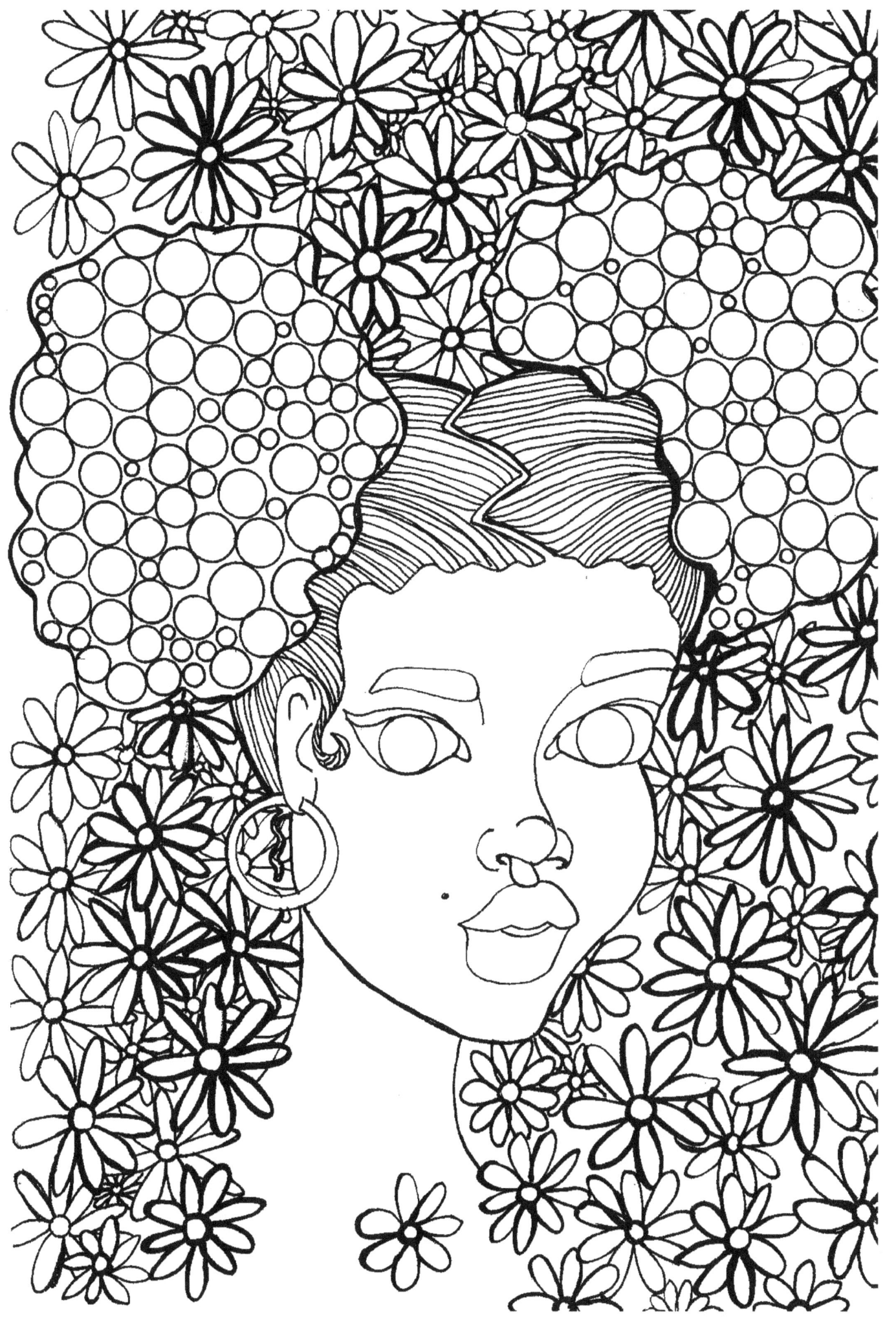

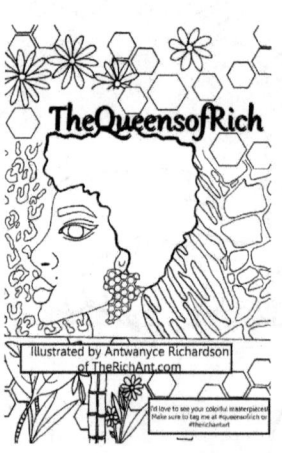

TheQueensofRich

Illustrated by Antwanyce Richardson
of TheRichAnt.com

I'd love to see your colorful masterpiece!
Make sure to tag me at #queensofrich or
#therichantart

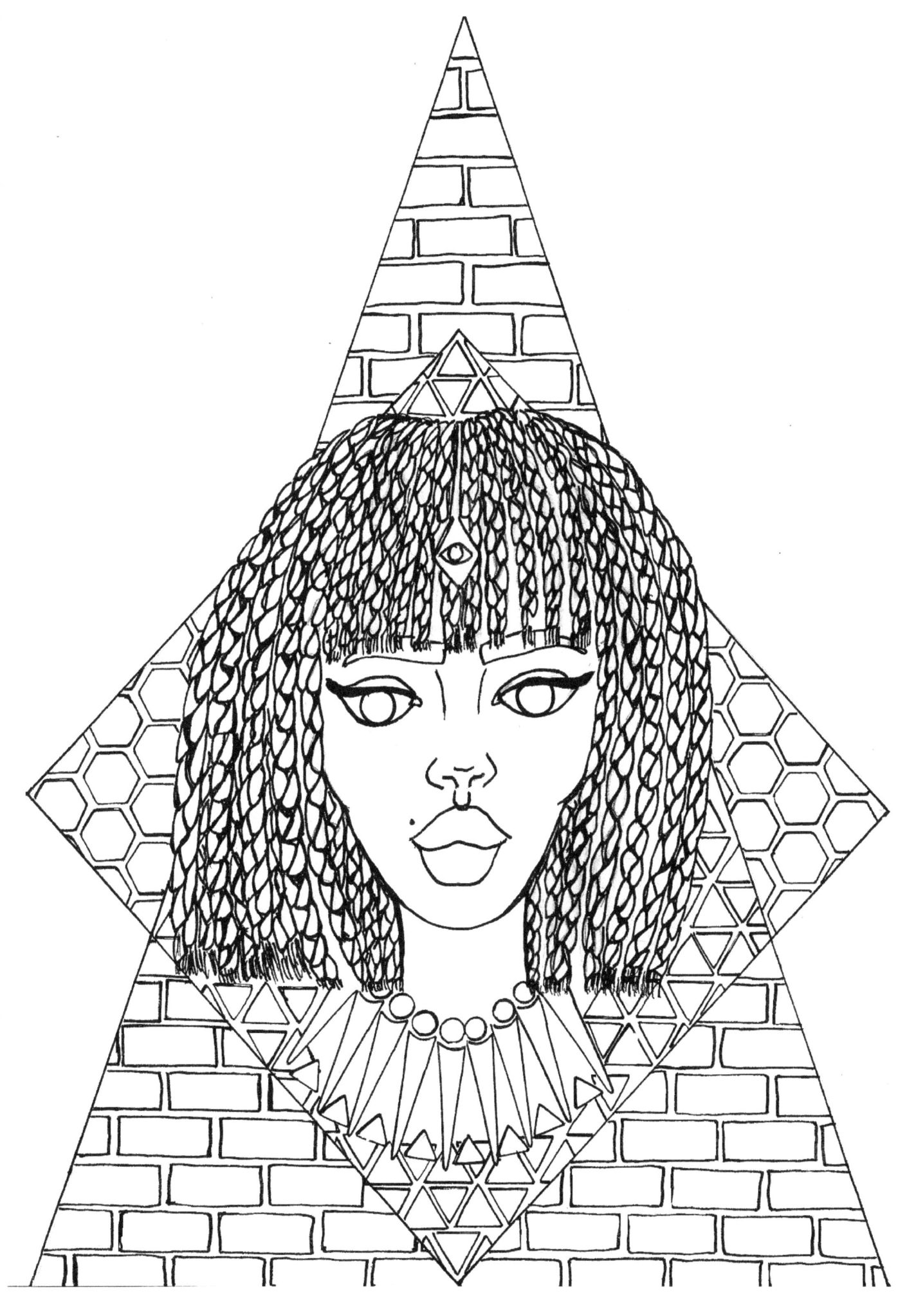

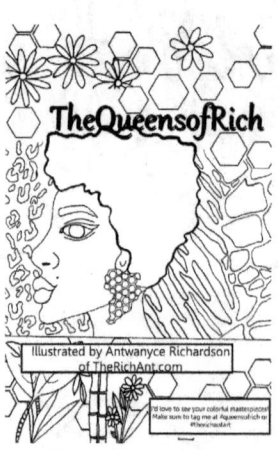

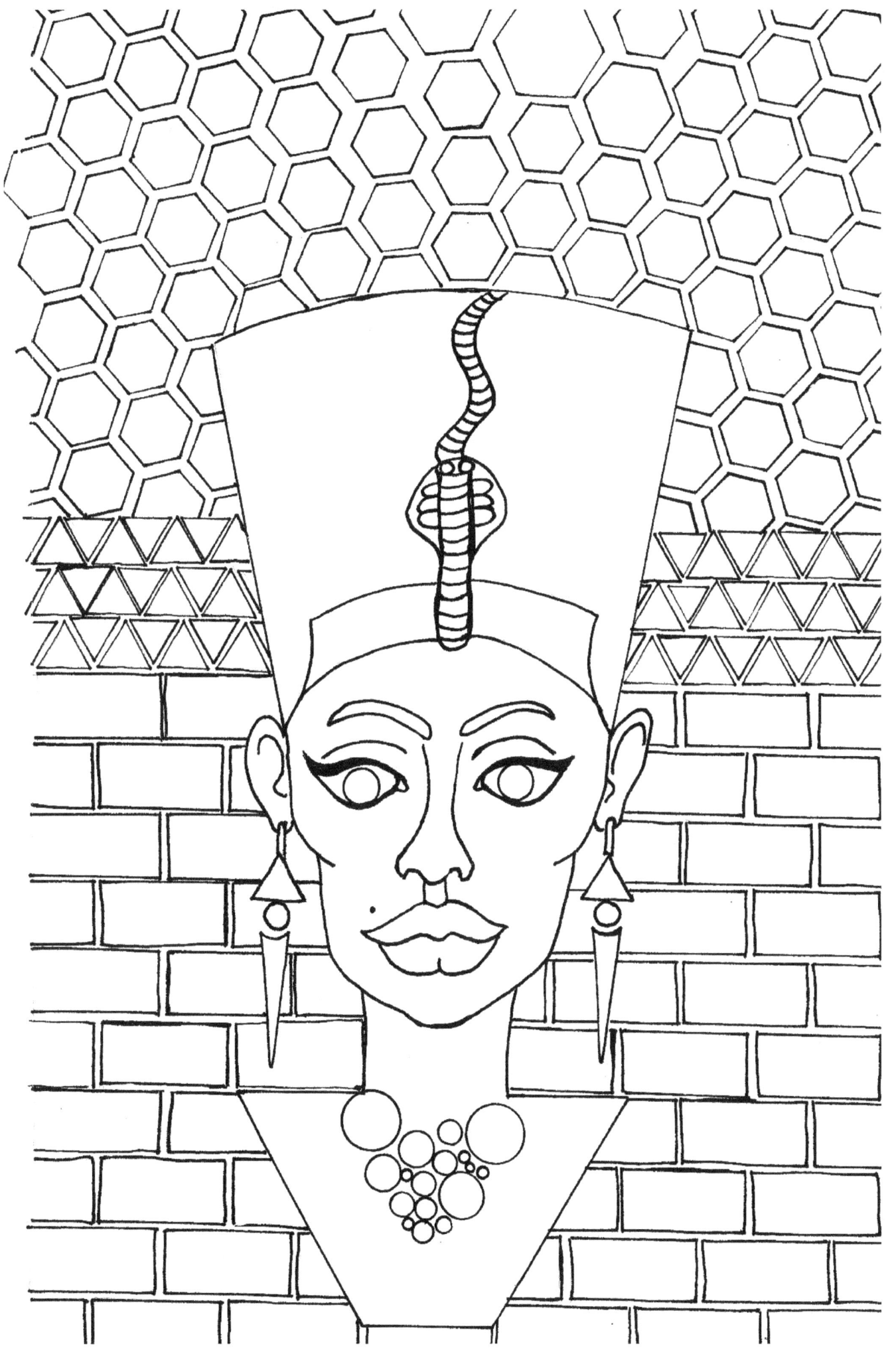

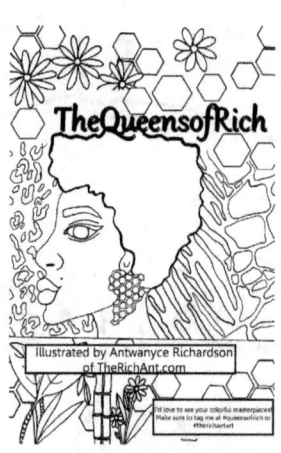

TheQueensofRich

Illustrated by Antwanyce Richardson
of TheRichAnt.com

I'd love to see your colorful masterpieces!
Make sure to tag me at #queensofrich or
#therichantart

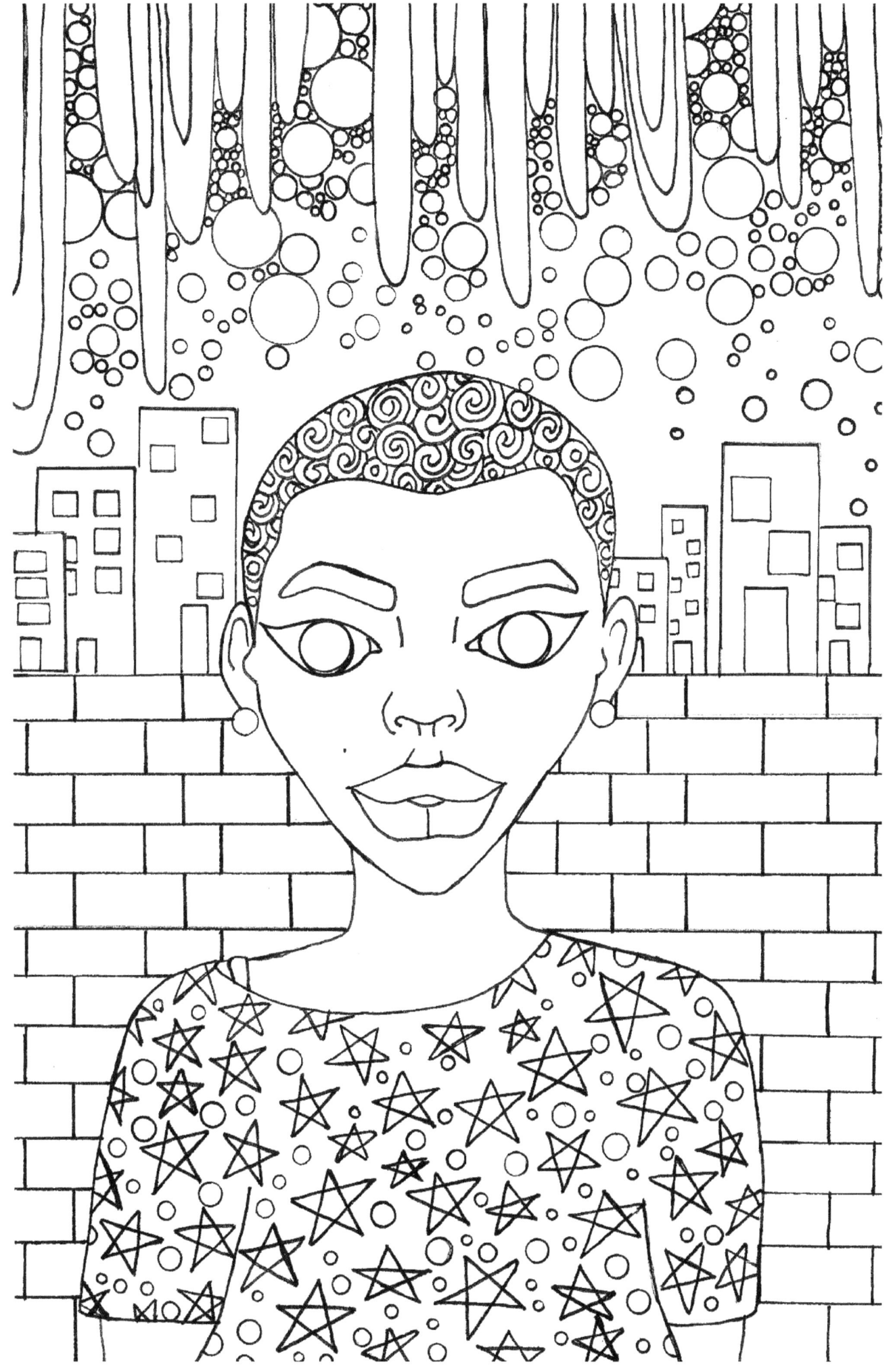

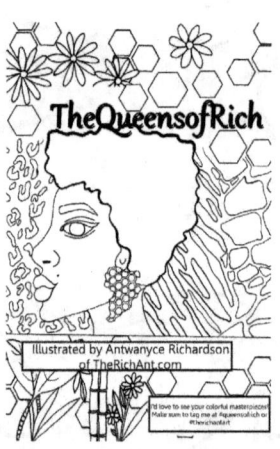

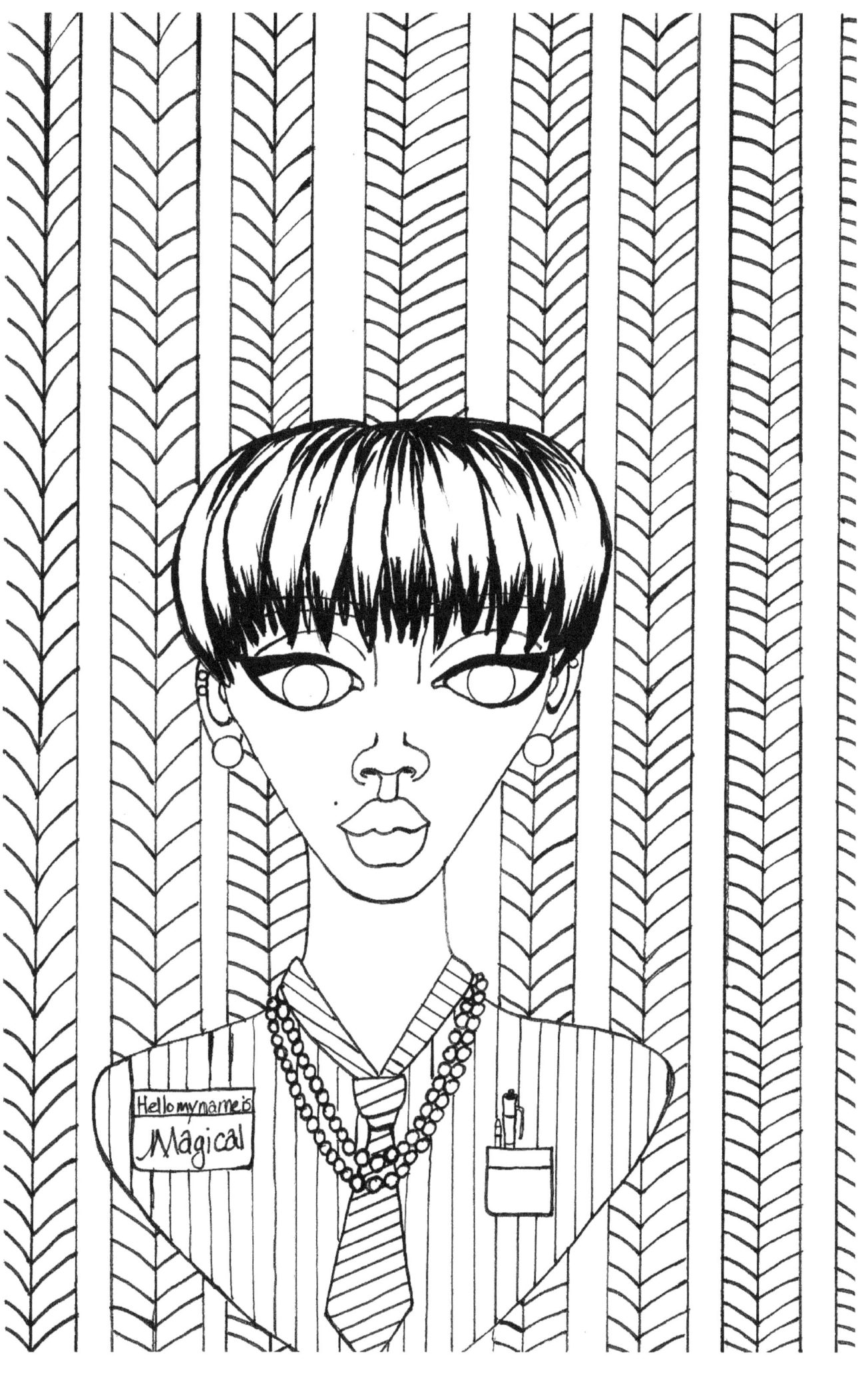

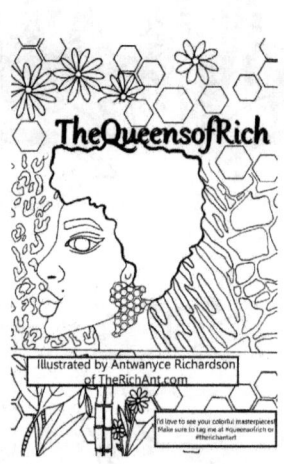

TheQueensofRich

Illustrated by Antwanyce Richardson
of TheRichAnt.com

I'd love to see your colorful masterpieces!
Make sure to tag me at #queensofrich or
#therichantart

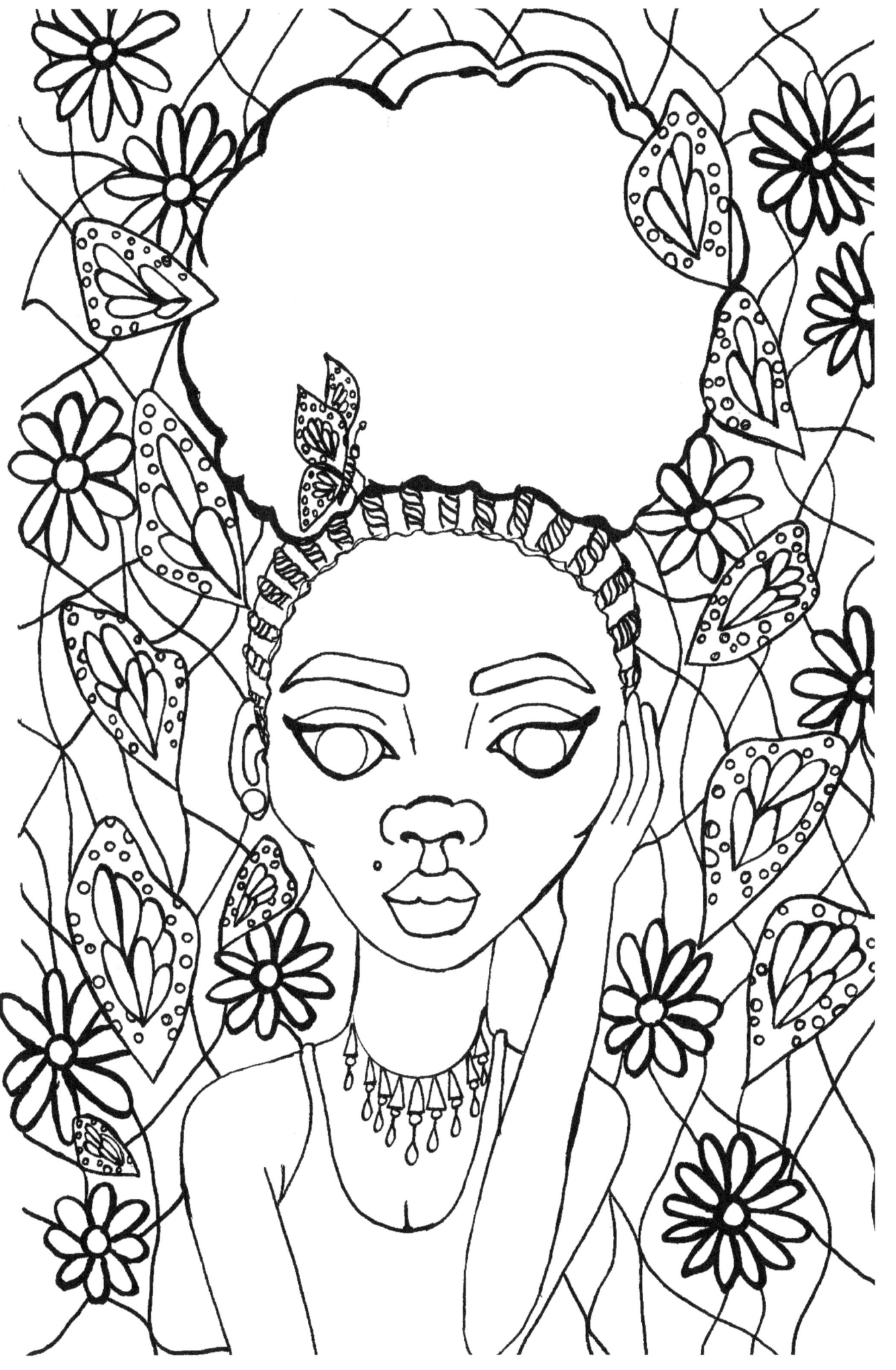

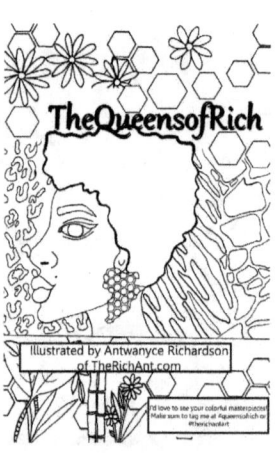

TheQueensofRich

Illustrated by Antwanyce Richardson
of TheRichAnt.com

I'd love to see your colorful masterpieces!
Make sure to tag me at @queensofrich or
#TheRichAntArt

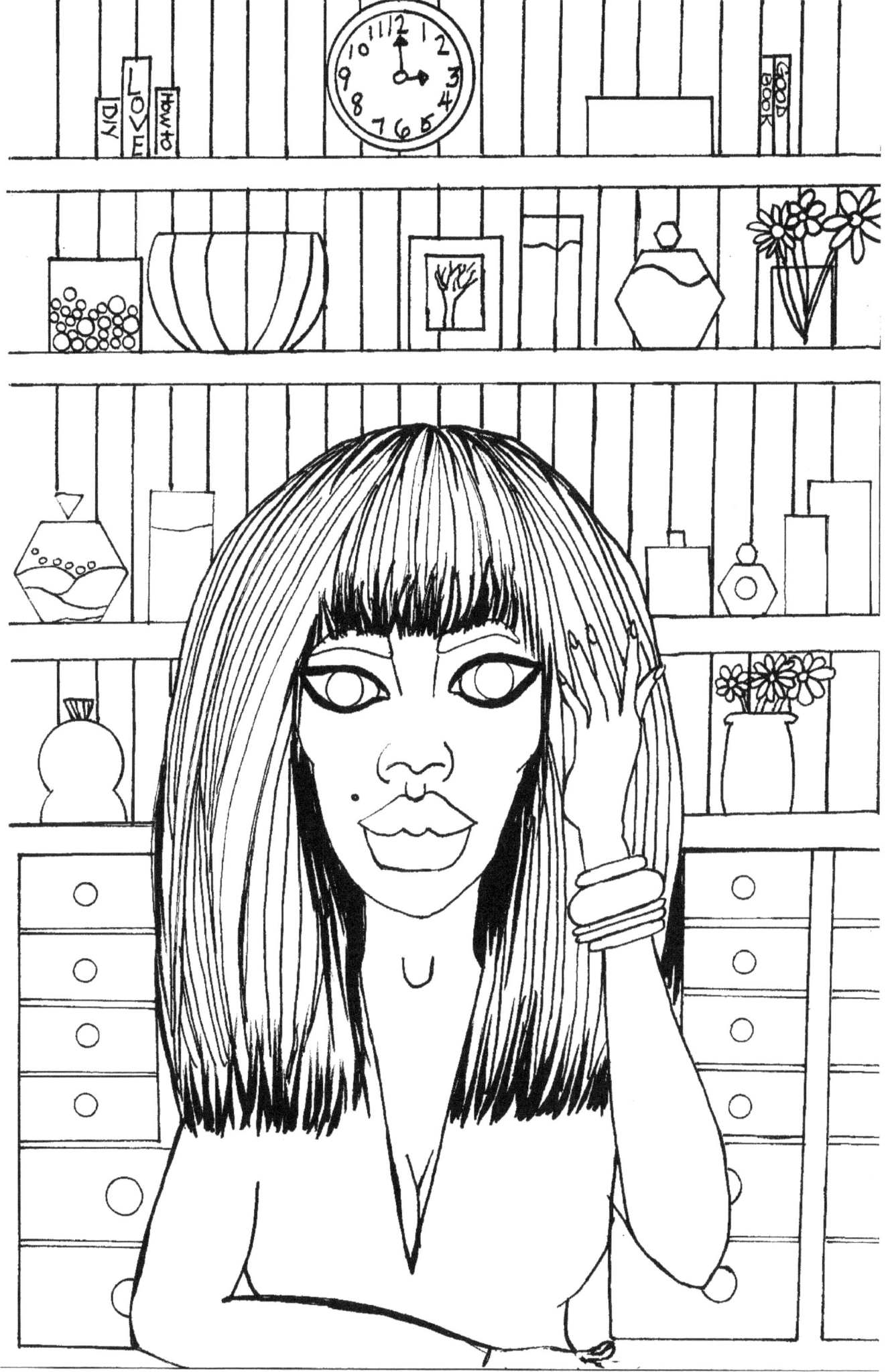

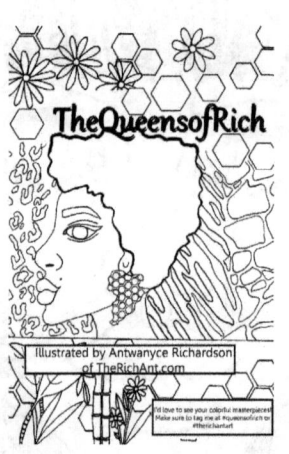

TheQueensofRich

Illustrated by Antwanyce Richardson
of TheRichAnt.com

I'd love to see your colorful masterpieces!
Make sure to tag me at #queensofrich or
#therichantart

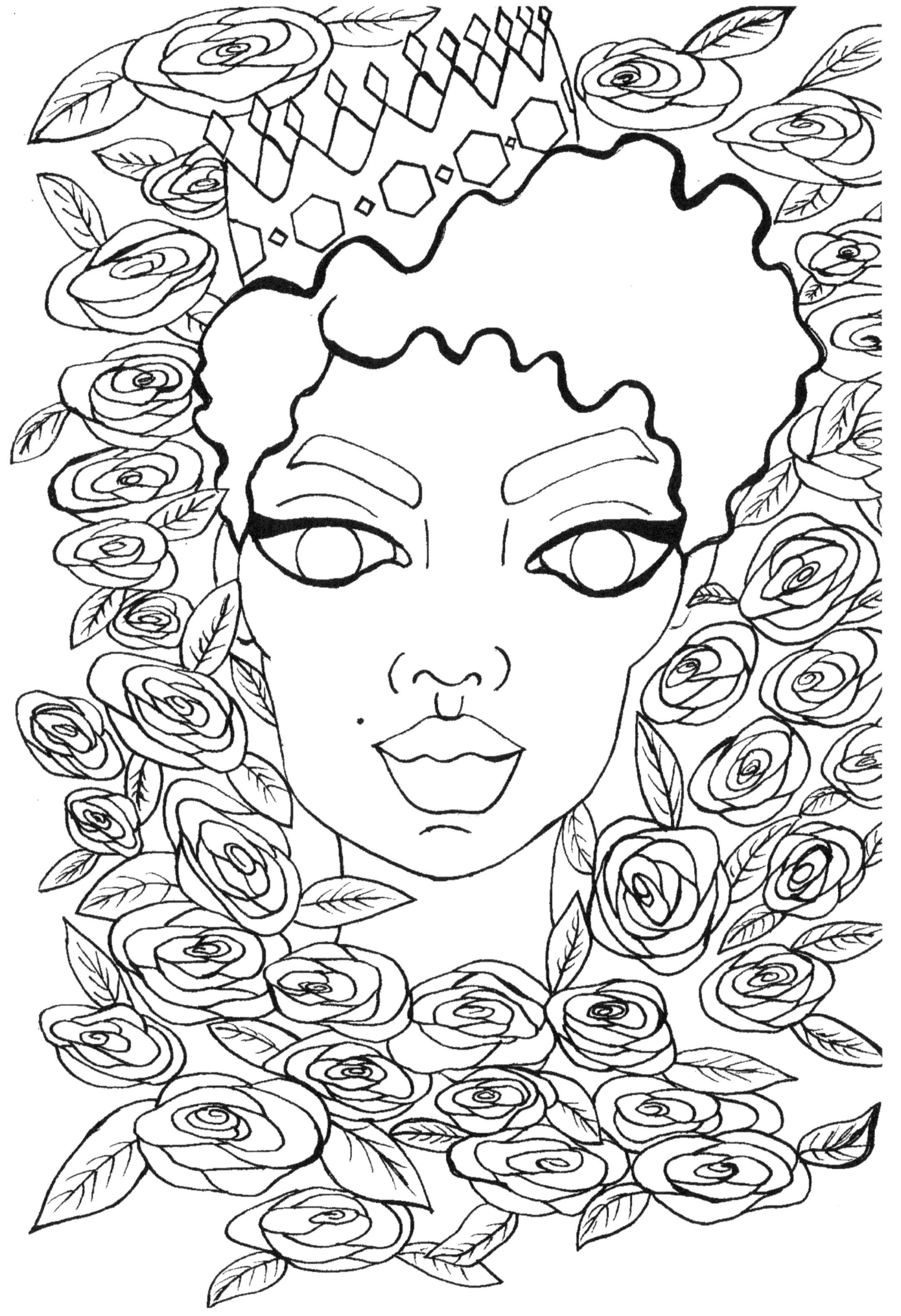

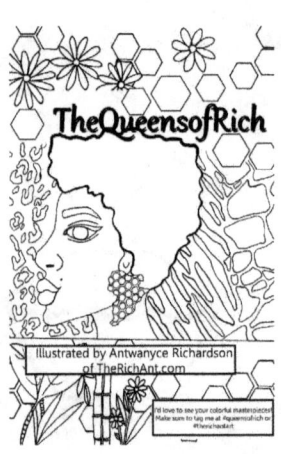

TheQueensofRich

Illustrated by Antwanyce Richardson
of TheRichAnt.com

I'd love to see your colorful masterpieces!
Make sure to tag me at #queensofrich or
#therichantart

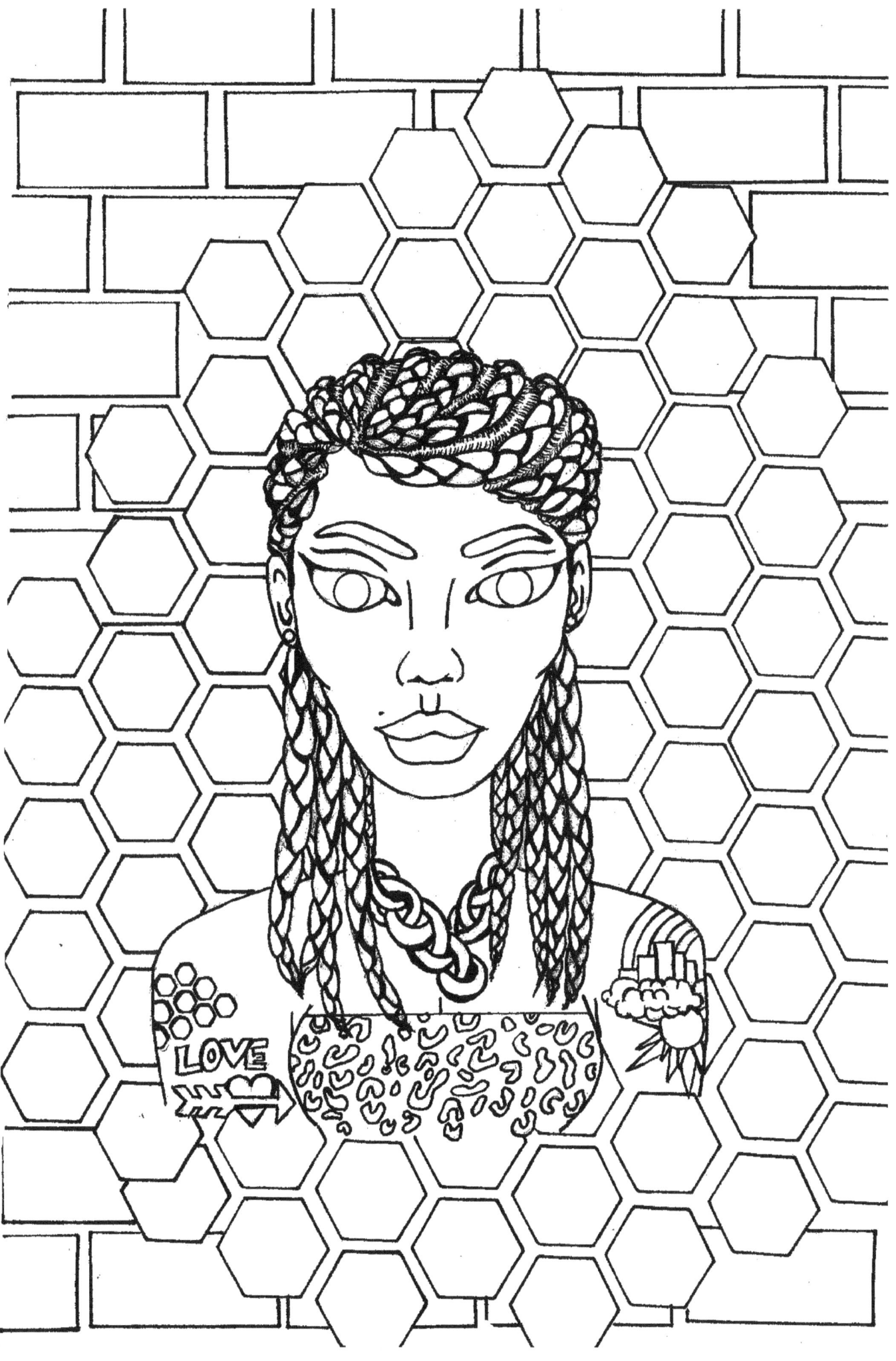

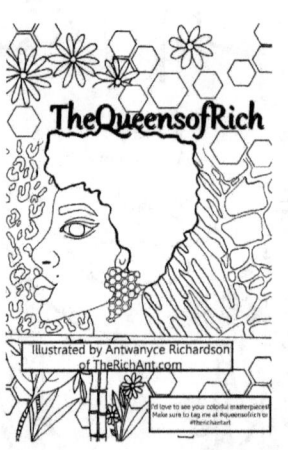

TheQueensofRich

Illustrated by Antwanyce Richardson
of TheRichAnt.com

I'd love to see your colorful masterpieces!
Make sure to tag me at #queensofrich or
#therichantart

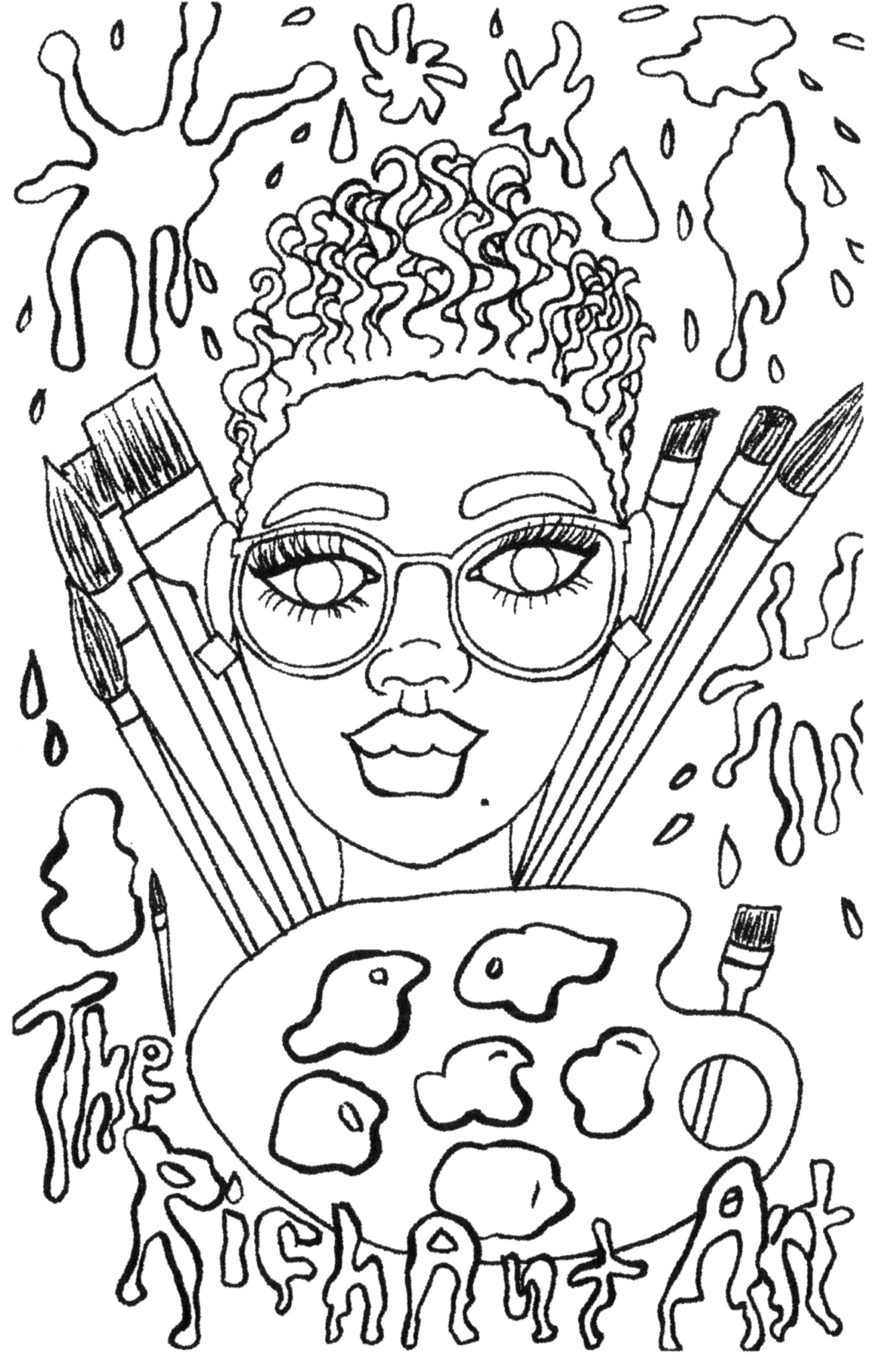

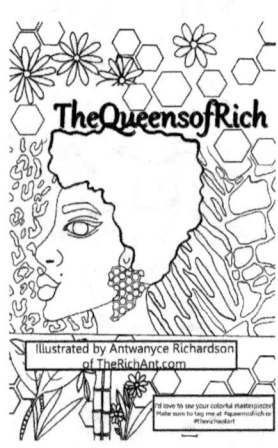

STAY TUNE FOR
VOLUME #2.
SISTERS ON TOUR.
SHOWCASING WOMEN
OF COLOR ON TRAVEL!

www.ingramcontent.com/pod-product-compliance
Lightning Source LLC
Chambersburg PA
CBHW080600190526
45169CB00007B/2831

9 781530 502929